TOTAL DEVASTATION

The Story of Hurricane Katrina

BY MICHAEL BURGAN

Consultant:
Richard Bell, PhD
Associate Professor of History
University of Maryland, College Park

CAPSTONE PRESS
a capstone imprint

Tangled History is published by Capstone Press,
1710 Roe Crest Drive, North Mankato, Minnesota 56003
www.mycapstone.com

Library of Congress Cataloging-in-Publication Data
Names: Burgan, Michael, author.
Title: Total devastation : the story of Hurricane Katrina / by Michael Burgan.
Other titles: Tangled history.
Description: North Mankato, Minnesota : Capstone Press, [2017] | Series:
Tangled history | Audience: Ages 8-14. | Audience: Grades 4 to 6.
Includes bibliographical references and index.
Identifiers: LCCN 2016009137
ISBN 9781491484524 (library binding)
ISBN 9781491484562 (paperback)
ISBN 9781491484609 (ebook pdf)
Subjects: LCSH: Hurricane Katrina, 2005—Juvenile literature. | Hurricanes—Juvenile
literature. | Disaster relief—United States—Juvenile literature. | Rescue work—
United States—Juvenile literature.
Classification: LCC HV636 2005 .U6 B87 2017 | DDC 363.34/92209763—dc23
LC record available at http://lccn.loc.gov/2016009137

Editorial Credits
Adrian Vigliano, editor; Heidi Thompson, designer; Svetlana Zhurkin, media
researcher; Tori Abraham, production specialist

Photo Credits
AP Photo: Dave Martin, cover, Robert F. Bukaty, 91; FEMA: Andrea Booher, 72, Jocelyn
Augustino, 92, Marty Bahamonde, 61, 86, Win Henderson, 42; Getty Images: NOAA,
4, The Boston Globe/Dina Rudick, 53; Newscom: EPA/Chris Graythen, 13, EPA/Sean
Gardner, 81, Reuters/Frank Polich, 27, Reuters/Marc Serota, 6, 36, Reuters/Rick
Wilking, 34, Sipa Press/Charley Varley, 99, UPI/A.J. Sisco, 19, 20, 24, UPI/Roger L.
Wollenberg, 77, UPI/Vincent Laforet, 56, ZUMA Press/Gary Coronado, 101

Printed in Canada.
009630F16

TABLE OF CONTENTS

FOREWORD

On August 26, 2005, residents of New Orleans, Louisiana, kept an eye on weather reports as they wondered if an approaching hurricane would hit their city and affect their lives. Along with other people in the Gulf of Mexico and Atlantic regions, they were several months into hurricane season. So far tropical storms as well as several hurricanes had already come and gone. In July, two hurricanes, Dennis and Emily, had blown through. These storms had taken lives and caused damage in surrounding areas, but so far New Orleans— and most of the United States—had been spared.

Local, state, and federal officials also watched the weather reports. They had the responsibility of deciding if a storm was severe enough that people should leave their homes and seek safety away from the coast.

At the National Hurricane Center in Miami, Florida, meteorologists stared intently at their computer screens, looking at satellite images and data. On a wall next to them, a large map showed the United States with the Atlantic and Pacific Oceans on either side. Off the west coast of the southern end of Florida was a red marker that stood for Hurricane Katrina. It had just crossed into the Gulf of Mexico from Florida as a Category 1 storm. That meant Katrina was the least powerful kind of hurricane, with wind speeds between 74 and 95 miles per hour. The most powerful hurricane, a Category 5, would have sustained winds of more than 156 miles per hour—strong enough to destroy homes and uproot most trees in its path.

The meteorologists analyzed data on the storm and kept watching their computers. There was no way to be sure which direction Katrina would go or how powerful it would become.

A GROWING STORM

1

Max Mayfield

Max Mayfield, the director of the
National Hurricane Center, kept a
close watch on Hurricane Katrina
as it approached the Gulf Coast. He
wanted to know what the storm's next
moves would be. During his career
as a meteorologist, he had seen many
powerful hurricanes pound the coasts
of the United States. In 1992 he
had tracked Hurricane Andrew as it
devastated parts of Florida. Andrew
was one of only three Category 5
storms in moderm times to come
ashore in the country. Its top wind
gusts reached at least 175 miles per
hour, knocking out instruments the
center used to measure the storm.

When it was over, Andrew had directly killed 26 people. Several dozen more died indirectly, from causes such as heart attacks suffered while trying to cope with the storm. Andrew also left an estimated 250,000 people homeless and caused about $25 billion in damage.

Mayfield knew the dangers of a storm like Andrew. But Katrina did not seem to pose the same threat—at least not at first. After hitting Florida, its winds weakened, making it a tropical storm rather than a hurricane. But the weakening didn't last. Starting in the early hours of August 26, the storm reached the warm waters of the Gulf of Mexico. Storms typically gain energy from the heat in those waters, and Katrina was no different. As it moved northwest, it became a Category 2 hurricane with winds of around 100 miles per hour. Mayfield knew the storm would strengthen even more. And as he followed its movement, he thought it might be on track to hit New Orleans, Louisiana.

That afternoon, Mayfield called his friend Walter Maestri, who lived just west of New Orleans in Jefferson Parish. Maestri was the official in charge of preparing the parish's residents for emergencies.

"This is it," Mayfield told his friend. "This is what we've been talking about all of these years." Mayfield and other hurricane experts had predicted that a powerful hurricane could hit New Orleans directly, causing extreme damage. With the city sitting so close to the Gulf of Mexico, and with some areas below sea level, experts worried that a Category 4 or 5 storm could create a storm surge that would ruin parts of the city.

"Are you kidding me?" Maestri asked.

His surprise made sense. Mayfield knew that many previous reports had said Katrina was tracking up Florida's west coast, not near New Orleans.

"No, Walt," Mayfield replied. "This is real." Mayfield called Louisiana state officials too. He wanted them to prepare for what was coming their way.

Vien The Nguyen

August 26, Mary Queen of Vietnam
Church, New Orleans

In the morning, before starting the day's
work, Father Vien The Nguyen sat in front
of his TV and watched the news. A weather
report mentioned a hurricane that had just hit
parts of southern Florida.

"Katrina made landfall last night near
Miami," the announcer said. "Winds
reached 80 miles per hour but the storm
has now weakened and seems to be heading
for Florida's northern coast." Nguyen, an
immigrant from Vietnam, was sorry to hear
the storm was heading to that region. Another
storm had just hit there and residents were
still trying to get back on their feet.

But Nguyen didn't have much time
to think about the weather. His church,
Mary Queen of Vietnam, had thousands

of members, all of them originally from Vietnam and neighboring countries. His days were filled with saying mass and helping his parishioners solve personal problems. His thoughts turned to the evening, when he would be attending a wake, and the next day when he'd say mass at the burial.

Renee Martin

August 27, the West Bank area, New Orleans

Renee Martin had already heard that a hurricane might be heading toward New Orleans, but she, like many other residents, didn't pay too much attention. It seemed that whenever the weather forecast said a storm was coming their way, it lost strength or turned away from the city. That had happened just the year before. In September 2004, hundreds of thousands of people evacuated the region as Hurricane Ivan roared through the Gulf of Mexico. The Category 4 storm's path had drifted west, meaning it could hit New Orleans. In the end, the storm veered to the east, and its full force missed the city.

Still, Martin knew the damage hurricanes could do to her adopted home. She had been born in Hawaii and had a mixed racial background: part Japanese, part white, part Hispanic, part African American. Her family settled in New Orleans in 1964, when she was about 6. The next year, Hurricane Betsy blew through with winds reaching 145 miles per hour. The part of the city where her family lived flooded, and for a time they didn't have food or electricity. Years later, Martin still recalled the image of dead bodies floating in the flooded streets.

But Betsy was in the past, and Martin was not worried about Katrina, even though she lived alone and was not feeling well. After two back surgeries, she still suffered tremendous pain. The medication doctors gave her for it made her sick. But when she stopped taking it, she felt sick too. Still, she didn't want to take the drugs and had stopped about two weeks earlier.

Throughout the day, Martin continued to hear that Katrina could be coming toward New Orleans. She remembered when city officials had urged people to evacuate for Ivan, though it hadn't been mandatory. This time, Martin didn't hear anything about evacuating. She stayed alone in her apartment.

New Orleans residents try to evacuate the city before Hurricane Ivan in 2004.

Peter Ward

Peter Ward spent part of Saturday morning watching TV. The station featured Jefferson Parish's emergency management director, Walter Maestri, warning of Katrina's growing strength. Thanks to his job, Ward knew something about the damage hurricanes caused in the Gulf Coast area. He operated a boat for Louisiana State University, and he sometimes carried scientists who studied the effects of storms on the environment.

"This doesn't sound good," Ward said to his wife.

"What's the matter?" she asked.

"I don't feel right about this hurricane," Ward said. "Something in my gut says it's going to be a bad one."

"What should we do?"

"I think we should evacuate."

The Wards began gathering up important papers and got ready to leave for Dallas, Texas. They knew it would be best to go before the roads became clogged with other people fleeing the city.

"You should go now, alone," Ward suggested, realizing how long it would take him to finish preparing the house for the hurricane. "I'll meet you in Dallas as soon as I'm done here."

He wanted to board up the house windows so Katrina's wind wouldn't blow out the glass. He also wanted to move valuable items off the floor in case the house flooded.

"Don't worry about me," Ward told his wife as she got into her car. "I'll see you tomorrow."

Vien The Nguyen

After the morning's burial mass, Father Nguyen headed to West Bank, a part of New Orleans on the west side of the Mississippi River. As he traveled to a meeting there, he listened to the radio. He heard the announcer say,

"Katrina seems to be heading our way."

As the day went on, Nguyen tried to stay alert for updates about the approaching storm. He said an evening mass, then attended a celebration at the church. But even with the party going on around him, Nguyen was thinking about Katrina and his parishioners' safety. He told those who could leave the city that they should: "Get out as quick as possible. Don't wait until tomorrow." Nguyen, though, would not be joining them. He had masses to say on Sunday. And he knew some people would not be able to leave the city. He wanted to be there to help them if Katrina did hit.

Max Mayfield and the other meteorologists
continued to watch Katrina strengthen as
the storm blew toward Louisiana. During the
morning, it reached Category 3 status. This
meant its winds were hitting more than 110
miles per hour. Mayfield believed that the
hurricane would soon become a Category 4,
and might even reach Category 5.

At noon, he joined a videoconference call
with the Washington, D.C., office of the
Federal Emergency Management Agency
(FEMA). The agency was in charge of helping
Americans cope with a range of emergencies,
from natural disasters to terrorist attacks.
Disaster specialists from the Gulf Coast states
also took part. Mayfield knew they understood
the dangers a storm like Katrina presented.
But he wanted to make sure other government
agencies that worked with FEMA knew too.

"This is no drill," Mayfield said. Then, wanting to make sure everyone on the call understood that Katrina was different from other powerful hurricanes, he continued: "It's strong, but it's also much, much larger."

"What's the danger for New Orleans?" someone from FEMA asked.

Mayfield explained that the storm surge could go higher than the dikes and levees meant to protect the city from floods. He hoped the experts hearing this understood that Katrina could be the much-predicted "Big One"—the hurricane powerful enough to wipe out New Orleans.

Throughout the day, Mayfield kept spreading the message of the danger Katrina posed. He talked to reporters from New Orleans' largest newspaper and he appeared on cable news. His basic message was, "This is really scary." He knew Katrina could still veer away from New Orleans as Ivan had done. But all the data the hurricane center had collected convinced Mayfield otherwise. He felt sure the storm would hit land either at or very close to New Orleans.

Mayfield also called the governors of Louisiana and Mississippi, to make sure they understood the dangers ahead. Louisiana governor Kathleen Blanco had already suggested—but not required—that residents in low-lying areas evacuate. New Orleans mayor Ray Nagin had joined her when she made the statement. But Blanco told Mayfield she wasn't sure Mayor Nagin really understood how bad Katrina could be. So Mayfield called Nagin, who was out to dinner with his wife. Mayfield said: "Mr. Mayor, I've never seen a storm like this. I think you should order a mandatory evacuation—now."

Louisiana governor Kathleen Blanco asked residents of New Orleans to make plans for a possible evacuation as Katrina approached.

CATEGORY 5

2

As Katrina approached, people boarded up windows and did whatever else they could to prevent homes, businesses, and public buildings from being damaged.

Tony Zumbado

August 28, Homestead, Florida

Tony Zumbado wasn't surprised that morning when the phone rang. He had been watching the reports and knew that a growing storm was crossing the Gulf of Mexico and heading for New Orleans. As he expected, the call was from NBC News.

Zumbado was a videographer and often shot videotape for the network, especially of hurricanes. Just a few days before, he had recorded the effects of Katrina in South Florida. Now NBC wanted Zumbado and sound engineer Josh Holm to head to New Orleans. The two men were soon on the road and heading west.

21

As they approached Louisiana, Zumbado had a strange feeling—something wasn't right. "I wonder where they're at?" he said to Holm.

"Who?" Holm asked.

"The emergency teams. The power crews to fix the electrical lines. They should be heading in now."

After almost 30 years of covering storms, Zumbado knew what to expect. He knew that emergency crews headed to a potential storm site before a hurricane hit. But not this time.

Reaching New Orleans, another thing struck Zumbado. In this type of situation, police would typically be on the streets trying to keep people out of a low-lying area like New Orleans. But Zumbado didn't see any officers. Then, at the hotel where he and Holm were staying, Zumbado was surprised again. Usually hotels emptied out as a hurricane neared because guests evacuated. This hotel was full. It seemed that people had not left New Orleans even though Mayor Nagin had called for a mandatory evacuation early that morning. There seemed to be local people as well as tourists at the hotel. Perhaps the locals had no way to leave the city and thought it might be safer in the hotel than in their homes. Based on what he had learned from covering storms in Florida, Zumbado could see that New Orleans was not ready for Katrina.

Max Mayfield
August 28, The National Hurricane Center, Miami

Just before noon, Max Mayfield prepared for another videoconference with FEMA and local emergency officials. Michael Brown, the director of FEMA, had arranged the call. After they got started, Brown announced that President George W. Bush was joining the call.

With the president now listening too, Mayfield went ahead and began sharing the bad news. That morning, Katrina had become a Category 5 storm with winds of about 167 miles per hour, and its track was still taking it right toward New Orleans. "I don't have any good news here at all today." Mayfield said. He explained the storm's strength, size, and path, and noted that the particular danger for New Orleans was the storm surge. At Lake Pontchartrain, which bordered New Orleans to the north, the storm surge could push water over the levees.

Later in the call, Brown shared his concerns with Mayfield and the others. He worried that New Orleans had only one large shelter available, at the Superdome. He also wondered if its roof would survive Category-5-force winds. Like Mayfield, he said Katrina would be "a bad one and a big one."

Downtown New Orleans began to look deserted on August 28 as Katrina neared the city.

As Katrina neared New Orleans, Ivory Clark didn't think evacuating was an option. As a chef at a restaurant in the city's main business district, he had to be available over the weekend. He also had a mother-in-law who was 91 and not in good health. Clark wouldn't think of leaving her behind, but he thought she was too old to stand a long, hot drive out of state.

Clark spent the morning helping friends put wooden boards over the windows of their homes. Then he went to pick up his mother-in-law and take her to his family's house. Seven people, including Clark's own family, an aunt, and a niece, now sought safety in the house. But when Clark heard Katrina had become a Category 5 hurricane, he thought the family might be safer in a motel. The family packed into their car and headed out.

The Clarks drove through the city trying to find a place with a room. It took an hour or so, but finally they found one at the Grand Palace Hotel. The name didn't accurately describe the place, which was a little run down. But the family didn't have much choice. They settled in with the fast food and snacks they had brought to feed them during the storm. Clark hoped the family would be all right there.

Peter Ward

August 28, Jefferson Parish, Louisiana

Preparing his house for the storm took Peter Ward most of Sunday. At 4:30 p.m., he got in his car to go join his wife in Texas, but the weather was getting bad. Katrina was still hours away, but the storm was already producing some wind and rain. Ward knew it would only get worse. Before Ward left, a police officer who lived nearby asked if he could borrow one of Ward's large business trucks.

The officer said, "With that raised body and those big wheels, it could be good to use in a flood."

"Sure," Ward said. "As matter of fact, I'll take another one and go with you. I think it's too late for me to head to Texas."

The two men, along with another officer, drove three trucks to a police station in the city and then took shelter in a small brick-and-concrete building nearby. They hoped it would be strong enough to survive the storm.

People run for cover as Katrina's high winds blow pieces of metal through the air.

Courtney Miles

Courtney Miles got ready to leave his grandmother's, where he lived, and head to his girlfriend Jamie's house. "I'll be back later tonight," the 18-year old told his grandmother.

Miles hadn't known much about Katrina, but he soon learned. That evening, as he and Jamie watched TV, the power went out. As strengthening winds began to rattle the apartment's windows, Jamie's mother told him to stay the night. Miles worried about his grandmother being alone. She had taken care of him for years, while his mother spent time in jail for selling drugs. Their neighborhood was poor and violence was common, but Miles tried to stay out of trouble. His religious beliefs and focusing on basketball helped.

He decided to stay at Jamie's and soon fell asleep on the floor. Around 2:00 a.m., thunder woke him. He hoped his grandmother was all right.

Peter Ward
August 29, New Orleans

Early in the morning, Peter Ward woke up in the shelter he and the officers had found. Katrina was raging all around them. They went outside to see the storm's full force. They watched as the winds ripped an air-conditioning unit off the roof of a nearby hospital.

"Watch out!" one of the officers yelled. The unit landed at their feet and broke into pieces. But before any of the fragments could hit them, the wind blew them away.

"This is crazy," Ward said. "Let's get inside." The officers quickly agreed. They might not be so lucky the next time something flew into the street.

Father Nguyen woke up several times in the early hours of Monday morning. On Sunday, about 120 parishioners had come seeking shelter in the second story of a new building at the church. It was tall enough to keep them safe from flooding, and Nguyen hoped it would also be strong enough to survive high winds. He spent the night in his house, waking up once to hear the wind slamming against the windows. Later, he heard the sound of water. The wind was pushing rain through a crack in the window sill.

"At least we still have power," Nguyen said to himself, as he heard the news playing on his television: "Katrina is now a Category 4 storm, with winds around 150 miles per hour."

Nguyen got up, mopped up the water, and placed a bucket to catch what was still coming in. A little while later, the lights went out. Katrina had finally knocked out the power. Nguyen heard the wind shake his house so hard the building creaked in the darkness.

Renee Martin
August 29, Lakeview, New Orleans

On Sunday, Renee Martin had heard that Katrina was strengthening, so she took shelter with a friend in Lakeview, another part of New Orleans. Martin thought she would be safer there. She and her friend heard the rain and wind all through Sunday night into the early hours of Monday.

"Hear that?" Martin asked. Her friend nodded. The wind was picking up everything loose in the streets and sending it crashing into the house. Martin curled up in a corner of the house and prayed.

Her friend's apartment was in the basement of the building. In the morning, as the storm died down, she lay on the bed. Getting up, she was surprised to find herself standing in knee-deep water.

"Renee!" Her friend called from another room. "There's water everywhere!"

"I know," Martin said, and the two women tried to move a computer and other valuables to higher ground. Then they heard on the radio: "There's been a breach in one of the levees. Water is flooding parts of the city. Get out now if you can!"

Despite the warning, Martin's friend wanted to stay in her home. Martin decided she would search for higher ground. She went outside and walked through the cold water, which was starting to cover cars in the street. She had grabbed a blanket and a pillow before she left, and now she waded through the water to the house next door. No one seemed to be around, so Martin figured they had already evacuated. She climbed the stairs up to their second-floor porch, which was above the still-rising water. As night came, she decided to stay on the porch. The power was out, and the only light came from the stars. With the water still rising, she fell asleep.

Deputy Police Superintendent Warren Riley saw his dispatchers hard at work. At City Hall, Riley had helped set up an emergency center for local, state, and federal officials to follow Katrina's path and effects. But he had returned to the station to be with his men.

In the early hours of this Monday morning, several inches of water were already filling some streets near the station. Riley soon learned of the trouble residents across the city faced. In their 911 calls they reported that wind had ripped roofs off homes and water was pouring over dikes. But the police could do nothing, because as Katrina reached full force, they had to stay safe in the station. Going out would have put their lives at risk.

One call caught the attention of everyone near the dispatcher who took it, because it came from another officer in the department. "It's Chris Abbott," the dispatcher said. "He lives near the 17th Street levee and it just broke. Water is flooding his house. He's in the attic now."

"How bad is it?" Riley asked. The dispatcher put the call on speaker so everyone could hear.

"The water is rising," Abbott said. He tried to sound calm, but Riley and the others heard his fear. "It was up to my waist … It's up to my neck. Listen, I can't get out."

Canal Street, downtown New Orleans, August 29, 2005

Courtney Miles woke up thinking about his grandmother. Jamie's building had survived Katrina so far. But what would it be like even a few blocks away? When he reached his grandmother's apartment, he called for her. No answer. He ran out into the yard and called to neighbors who were outside, "Anybody see Miz Geraldine?" No one had.

While Miles worried and wondered where she was, he gathered with some friends to listen to the radio. The news at first did not sound too bad. The announcer said that most of New Orleans was in good shape, considering the Category 4 winds Katrina had when it reached the city. But then more news came in, this time about the breach of one of the levees. The flooding was on the other side of the Mississippi River—not near Algiers, but Miles and his friends knew people there. And no one could say if the floodwaters might hit Algiers too. As he imagined the destruction in the other parts of New Orleans, Miles couldn't forget that he still didn't know what had happened to his grandmother.

Water floods into New Orleans through a broken levee after Katrina.

As Monday went on and Katrina moved farther north, the wind died down and the rain lightened. Tony Zumbado and Josh Holm got orders from NBC to go out and film the floodwaters now overtaking parts of the city. The 17th Street levee was one of several that had breached.

As Zumbado and Holm drove, they saw items such as shoes and toys floating in the streets. "Those are brand new," Zumbado said. "People must be looting the stores near here." Soon, the two men saw the proof—about 20 people were braving the floodwaters to enter a small store and steal anything they could grab. Zumbado filmed it, then the two men continued on. They found a police officer and told him about the looting. But his radio was out and his car was dead. The officer got in the van and saw the looting for himself.

Coming upon some other officers, the police worked together to run down some of the looters, though it was hard to run as the water was now several feet deep. Once again, Zumbado could not believe how unprepared New Orleans had been for Katrina. The officers didn't even have rain gear to wear. They also didn't know where to take the looters, since all the jails were flooded. Zumbado and Holm left as the officers debated what to do. They had more scenes of destruction and hardship to document.

Warren Riley

August 29, Police Department Headquarters, New Orleans

More officers gathered around to hear Chris Abbott's panicked voice. Also in the room was Pete Ward, who had come to the station with his police buddy. Deputy Superintendent Riley stood next to Captain Jimmy Scott as he took over the situation.

"Chris, do you have your gun?" Scott asked.

"Yeah," Abbott said.

Scott instructed Abbott to begin shooting holes into an attic vent, about an inch apart.

"The water's up to my chin," Abbott reported.

Scott kept talking, telling Abbott to shoot and then punch through the vent. Then he and his family could climb onto the roof and wait to be rescued.

Riley and the others heard several shots.

"Punch your way out!" Scott shouted.

"The water's up to my mouth," Abbott said. *"I'm halfway out, and I'm going to make*

Suddenly, the line went dead. An eerie silence fell over the room.

Vien The Nguyen
August 29, Mary Queen of Vietnam Church, New Orleans

By about 2:30 p.m., Father Nguyen thought the worst of Katrina was over. He drove through the neighborhood to see the effects of the storm. Trees were down everywhere and roofs were damaged, but there was little water in the street. When he went out later, though, he noticed something odd. Even though the rain had stopped, the water seemed to be rising. He made a mark on the side of a building. When Nguyen came back just a few minutes later, the mark was underwater.

Listening to his car radio, Nguyen heard the bad news: "We have reports of dikes and flood walls breaching all over the city." Nguyen realized that even though Katrina had passed, New Orleans was still facing a bad situation. Who knew how long water would continue pouring through the breached levees before they could be repaired? The city's low-lying areas would fill up like bowls.

A few hours later, the water on the street had risen to the headlights on the church's van. Borrowing a boat, Nguyen paddled through the flooded streets, looking for parishioners who might be trapped in their homes. He didn't find any so he returned to the church. People who had left the parish building when Katrina ended now came back because of the flood. One of these people was an old woman who needed a machine to breathe. With the power out, this machine ran on a generator. But how long could Nguyen keep the generator supplied with fuel?

With the storm over, Ivory Clark realized his family needed more food and water. He talked to people staying in the hotel and learned that the Superdome had been opened as a shelter. He also heard that many others had run out of supplies.

"I have to go to the grocery store," he told his wife, Donna.

"You know there are no stores open," she said.

"I know," Clark replied. "I'll break in if I have to. We have hungry children and old people here. They need to eat! They need water!"

Clark had never stolen anything from anyone, and never would have—but this was a crisis. He went to a store and headed back with as much food as he could carry. When he returned, Donna told him that a gang of thieves had stormed the hotel, taking jewelry and frightening everyone.

"It's not safe here," Clark said. "Tomorrow we'll go to the Superdome."

PROBLEMS EVERYWHERE

Volunteers pilot boats through flooded New Orleans streets, looking for people in need of rescue.

Peter Ward

Peter Ward, like everyone else in the police headquarters, figured Abbott was dead. But Ward hadn't stuck around to find out. As soon as the storm weakened, he was out in his truck trying to rescue people. With a trailer behind the vehicle, he carried people from flooded areas to dry streets. Once he dropped them off, they would be able to walk to the Superdome.

Along with some police officers, Ward made several trips to Memorial Medical Center to pick up medical supplies and bring them to other parts of the city. Early that morning, on a hospital run, he saw an amazing sight: A manhole cover blew off the street and into the air. A powerful burst of water followed. Then another cover blew off, then came more water.

Up and down the street the same thing seemed to be happening.

"What is going on?" Ward asked one of the police officers.

"No idea," the officer said. "But all that water can't be a good sign."

Soon the street by the hospital was flooded with water 2 feet deep.

Karen Wynn

August 30, Memorial Medical Center, New Orleans

Karen Wynn was groggy as she woke from her sleep, surprised by the call that meant she was needed in the emergency room. Wynn was the head nurse for the intensive care unit (ICU) at Memorial Medical Center. But why would they bother *her*, she wondered. Someone else must have been available to help. It was about 5:00 a.m. and the storm was long over. Wynn didn't think any new patients would be coming to the hospital. She had been there since Sunday since she was one of the essential staff members who would stay at the hospital as long as she was needed.

Since Monday morning, the staff had been dealing with broken glass throughout the hospital and pools of water on the floors. The hospital had lost power too, and now only generators kept important medical equipment running so severely sick patients could live.

Wynn ran from the part of the hospital where she was staying to the emergency room. She saw blood everywhere, coming from an elderly woman lying on a gurney.

"What happened?" Wynn asked.

The woman's grandson explained that she had been stabbed. "Because of the storm, the ambulances aren't running," the young man said. "I had to carry her here." Wynn and a doctor hooked the injured woman to a machine to help her breathe. Then they used ultrasound to see if the knife had reached her heart. Luckily, it hadn't. Wynn watched as hospital staff took the woman to the last bed available in the ICU.

Later in the day, Wynn and the other ICU nurses listened to a local radio station. They heard callers talk about the waters still rising across the city. One man described sitting in his attic, his house surrounded by 9 feet of water.

"And is the water rising anymore?" the radio host asked.

"Yes, it's steady rising."

Renee Martin
August 30, Lakeview, New Orleans

On Tuesday morning, Renee Martin was still on the empty porch she had found near her friend's house. Her body was covered with mosquito bites. As the morning went on, she saw small boats cruising up and down the flooded street. She began waving and shouting, "Over here, over here!"

A man steered over to the porch and helped her climb in the boat. He then picked up several other people before heading to the Superdome. Nearing the building, they found that some large logs blocked the street.

"I can't get the boat any closer," the man said. "You'll have to walk the rest of the way."

Martin got out of the boat and stepped into water up to her knees. She smelled gasoline. She saw fish in the water, along with dead bodies. But she had no choice other than to keep walking in the hope of reaching safety. Finally, she reached the ramp to the Superdome, where people were waiting to get inside.

"There's no room," someone shouted. "They let too many people in."

"The storm blew some of the roof off," someone else told Martin. "Parts of the building are flooded inside."

Martin didn't like the sound of all that. She wanted to stay on the ramp, in case a ride came that might take her somewhere safer. Meanwhile, others pushed and shoved against her, trying to get inside.

Marty Bahamonde

Marty Bahamonde knew how bad things were at the Superdome. He had reached New Orleans on Saturday night, making him the only Federal Emergency Management Agency (FEMA) representative in the city. Almost the entire time he had been in New Orleans, he had been watching events at the Superdome.

Even before Katrina hit, he had warned FEMA officials in Washington about the growing crisis. By Monday night, he had seen the number of evacuees at the dome reach 20,000—more than could be accommodated there. Medical providers did not have enough oxygen for the sick people who needed it, and more sick people were still coming, hoping to find treatment.

Bahamonde had also seen firsthand the water pouring through a broken levee. He knew that if water had merely risen above the top of the levee, the level would eventually go down. The flooding would stop. But with a breach like this, water would continue to rush out until the hole was plugged.

When he woke up on Tuesday morning, Bahamonde saw that some of the streets around the arena were filled with water. Wearing just tennis shoes and shorts, he walked through the still-rising waters from the dome to the nearby hotel where Mayor Nagin was staying. Bahamonde wanted to tell him that Michael Brown of FEMA and other government officials were on their way. They would soon be flying over the dome to check out the situation.

Back at the dome, Bahamonde talked to some of the National Guard troops working there.

"Man, the smell from in there is terrible," Bahamonde said.

"All the toilets are clogged," a National Guard member said. "People are going to the bathroom wherever they can."

Bahamonde knew the problem was not just the smell. People could get sick from the human waste. Food and water were also running low. Medics needed supplies. He had some hope when FEMA began sending more people to the dome to help. But Bahamonde knew the people there still faced a difficult time. And he was determined to be right there with them, doing what he could to help.

Warren Riley

August 30, Police Department Headquarters, New Orleans

Warren Riley received a frantic call from his girlfriend, who had evacuated to Houston. "Get out of there," she said. "They're shooting at helicopters, they're shooting at police, they're killing people. They killed the police chief!"

"What are you talking about?" Riley said. "They didn't kill Chief Compass. He is sitting right here. Do you want to talk to him?"

Riley knew the source of his girlfriend's panic. All sorts of wild tales were spreading around the city and reaching the media. Too often media outlets seemed to report on rumors without checking if they were true. One man had shot at a helicopter, Riley knew that was true, but he was soon arrested. Looters were not firing on police, as some media reports said. But people stranded in their attics sometimes fired shots, to let rescuers know where they were.

Riley also knew that reports had been circulating that some police officers had fled the city, rather than trying to deal with the emergencies Katrina created. It was true that some officers had evacuated. But many others had stayed and suffered from the storm too. He thought about Chris Abbott, the officer who had been trapped in his attic. Thankfully he had been rescued. But another officer was stuck on her roof with no food or water. Riley didn't know when she would be rescued. Katrina and the flooding it brought made life hard enough for Riley and his officers. The false reports swirling around didn't make his job any easier.

"Let's go!" Nancy Wynn called to her nurses
as she moved quickly through the ICU, helping
them prepare patients to leave the hospital.
The waters had risen steadily throughout the
day on Tuesday. Officials had now arranged
for helicopters to evacuate the sickest infants
and some elderly patients in the ICU. The
helicopters would land on a pad on the roof of
the hospital's parking garage.

Wynn and her nurses worked in stifling
heat. With no power, the hospital had lost
its air-conditioning the day before. Today the
temperature was somewhere in the mid–90s
and the humidity was high. Wynn tried to pull
back the boards that still covered some of the
windows. She hoped the storm had broken the
glass so she could let in fresh air, even if it was
hot and sticky.

Only a single elevator was working to carry

patients down to the level of the helicopter pad. It took so long to go down and return that some of the nurses and relatives of the patients began carrying the sick down the stairs. They placed the patients on blankets and then grasped the blankets' sides.

Loading one patient into the elevator, Wynn heard the sound of sloshing water. She realized it must be beginning to fill the bottom of the elevator shaft. Wynn had to assume that soon she and her staff would lose access to this last working elevator.

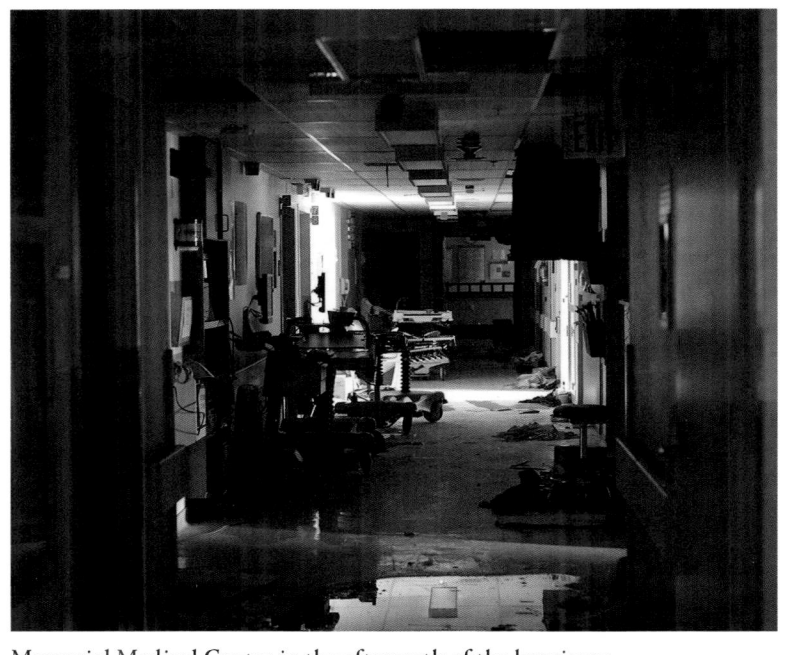

Memorial Medical Center in the aftermath of the hurricane

Sara Roberts

August 30, Lake Charles, Louisiana

Sara Roberts grew angry as she saw the news about the rising waters in New Orleans and the troubles at the Superdome. Roberts was an accountant in Lake Charles, a city in western Louisiana. But she had ties to New Orleans. The family of her husband, Andre Buisson, had deep roots there, and she served on the government commission that oversaw the Superdome and other event centers in Louisiana. So when the call came from Louisiana state official Sam Jones she was ready to help.

"We're not getting the aid we need from the federal government," Jones said. "Let's call out the volunteers. We've got to get those people out of New Orleans." Jones explained that he was looking for people who owned boats and could tow them into the city and work with state officials to evacuate people.

"I think I can do it," Roberts said.

She quickly called Ronny Lovett, a client of hers who owned a large construction company. She explained the idea of creating a "Cajun Navy" of private boats brought into New Orleans for rescue work. Roberts didn't know that Lovett had already been in touch with Roberts's husband to discuss a similar plan.

Lovett agreed to ask his employees if they had boats and if they were willing to help. Meanwhile, Roberts made calls to her friends. Before the morning was over, they had found 18 boats and 35 people willing to go to New Orleans. Lovett, who had done similar rescue work after Hurricane Andrew, made sure each boat had the right equipment, such as spotlights, chainsaws, and axes. The caravan would also be joined by one truck carrying extra fuel and another carrying water. When it came time to leave, Roberts and Buisson took the lead in their family's pickup truck. Buisson drove while Roberts sat beside him, her cell phone at the ready.

On the highway, others cars pulled over to let the Cajun Navy pass by, waving to the group. Roberts looked at her husband and said: "They know where we're going. They know we're going to help."

CHAOS AND HOPE

4

Some people were forced onto the roofs of buildings by rising water levels.

Ivory Clark

Although Ivory Clark had worried about his family's safety, they had stayed in their hotel room. But on Wednesday morning, Clark had a new concern. One of the people with him was his 72-year-old aunt Yvonne. She had asthma, and it had gotten worse. The machine she used to help her breathe needed electricity, but, as in much of the city, their area had lost power. Clark went into the flooded streets to look for help.

After spending a few hours outside, Clark spotted a man in a raft heading his way. He called out, "Please, mister, help me. I've got a really sick woman and a 90-year-old woman who can't walk."

"Bring 'em on," the man said.

The weight of the entire family made the rubber raft sink. The raft man got in the water and tugged it while Clark pushed from behind. Near the Superdome, they reached a dry spot. The family would have to walk the rest of the way. Clark knew his aunt and mother-in-law could not make the walk. He spotted a woman with a large grocery cart. Clark figured he could fit his elderly relatives inside—if the woman would give him the cart.

"Please, ma'am, can I have your cart? I have two women here who could die if they don't get proper food and medical help."

"I need this cart to move around my children," the woman said.

"They could die! Please," he pleaded.

"All right."

Clark quickly loaded the women into the cart and the family headed for the Superdome. When they reached it, Clark walked through the crowd outside to talk to some officials. Before he could reach them one of the men yelled, "The Superdome is closed. Go to the convention center." Clark went back to his family and told them they had more walking to do.

On Tuesday water had begun to fill some of the streets on the west side of the Mississippi River, where Courtney Miles lived. He and his friends had no way to evacuate—none of them owned a car. But even if they had a vehicle, there was no guarantee they could find streets that weren't flooded.

All that day, Miles had heard helicopters flying overhead. Now, on Wednesday afternoon, more buzzed through the skies. But no help came to his neighborhood. They didn't have any electricity or running water. Food was running low and the temperature was high. The situation left some people angry. Miles heard people arguing in the street. The situation would only get worse if they didn't get help.

"We can't even walk out," his friend Nas said. "I hear the police won't let people on foot cross the bridge."

"We need a car," his friend Jabbar said.

"No," Miles said. "What we need is a bus, a big ole bus to load up everybody and drive 'em out of here."

Miles knew where they could find a bus—the nearby lot where the city parked school buses. Miles, Jabbar, and Nas ran to the lot but found that the gate was locked. Luckily, Nas was small enough to slip through a gap in the fence and get inside.

"Start looking for keys," Miles said. He and Jabbar waited as Nas poked around the buses.

Finally Nas cried, "I found something! A box. And it has keys!" Nas came over to the fence. Miles took one of the keys and put it in the lock to the gate. The lock clicked open.

"We're in!" Miles said.

The teens then ran to different buses, looking for one that had gas. Finally, they found one with a full tank. Miles got behind the wheel. He didn't have his license, but his uncle had let him drive before. He hoped driving a bus would be like driving a car.

Many people had no choice but to travel through dirty floodwaters despite
the risk of skin infections and other diseases.

Marty Bahamonde kept in contact with various officials as he tried to keep the masses of people in the Superdome fed. Some portable military meals, called MREs, had arrived, but feeding people was still a struggle.

Bahamonde used his handheld device, a Blackberry, to send e-mails to Washington. In one message he wrote, "The situation is past critical ... thousands gathering in the streets with no food or water. Hundreds still being rescued from homes."

Bahamonde learned one piece of good news. Officials were planning to bring in buses to move people out of the Superdome. They would be taken to the Astrodome in Houston, Texas. But while he waited for the buses to arrive, people continued arriving at the Superdome, seeking help. To make

NEW   Juvenile   staff:_____

Call #   J976.044

BUR

Author   BURgan

Price   23.99

Sticker

Special Instructions

Type   blc

TAPE SPINE

363, 34

matters worse, Bahamonde knew that the media were reporting stories about murders going on inside the stadium. The stories were not true, but there had been fights and some people had died from untreated illnesses. Bahamonde feared even more would die if they weren't taken by medevac helicopters to hospitals that were still functioning.

Karen Wynn
August 31, Memorial Medical Center, New Orleans

As Wednesday began, Karen Wynn and her staff had completed their mission. They had evacuated all the ICU patients that needed to be moved. Just two patients remained. But any sense of relief faded quickly as Memorial's emergency generators failed. The building went dark and mostly silent.

Wynn spent some time that morning trying to sleep. When she couldn't relax, she got up to explore what was happening in other parts of the hospital. Another nurse, Thao Lam, saw Wynn and asked what she was doing.

Wynn said, "I'm not asleep, might as well get up and do something, be productive." Lam joined her as they used a flashlight to go down to the floor below. They soon found action, as more rescue helicopters were on their way. The two ICU nurses helped carry more patients to safety. Wynn touched several and felt how hot they were. Their medical conditions and the lack of air-conditioning had probably raised their temperatures to high levels She wondered how many of them would survive the trip out of the hospital.

Tony Zumbado
August 31, Morial Convention Center, New Orleans

Tony Zumbado and Josh Holm were planning their day of filming when a young man ran toward them. Zumbado tensed a bit, wondering if the guy might be on drugs or carrying a weapon. Instead, the man said, "I need to speak to somebody. There's people dying in the convention center."

"Let's go," Zumbado said. "Show me."

Zumbado, Holm, and the man, who said his

name was Dwayne Jones, drove to the nearby Morial Convention Center. When they got there, Zumbado could not believe the scene. People had been sleeping in the street. Elderly people who needed medical care sat in their wheelchairs. Trash was everywhere, and the whole area stank. Inside the center, the smell was even worse. As people called for help, needing food and water, Jones led Zumbado to a large freezer. Inside were the bodies of people who died while seeking shelter at the convention center.

By now anyone who had been watching the news knew about the conditions at the Superdome. But the outside world didn't know about these disgusting and dangerous conditions at the convention center.

As Zumbado filmed, Holm recorded the voices of some of the people inside. One man said, "They haven't eaten, they haven't had no water, they haven't had a bed to sleep, they haven't taken a bath. How are we going to survive out here?"

Another man said, "I mean, we might as well just lay down and die."

One woman could only cry "Help!" over and over. Another woman saw Zumbado filming and became angry. She thought Jones had brought someone who could help. Zumbado told her, "If you let me videotape this and you let me get out of here with this, I'll bring you help."

Ivory Clark

August 31, Morial Convention Center, New Orleans

When Ivory Clark reached the convention center, he was shocked. He had hoped to find a generator for his aunt's breathing machine, but instead he found a scene of chaos. Clark would not take his family inside the center, so they tried to sleep on the curb. After seeing several dead bodies wrapped in blankets, he decided they had to move on again.

Sara Roberts and her husband set off in the first boats from the Cajun Navy. She was soon stunned by the number of people in need. The first family she helped rescue included a woman who had lost contact with her sister.

"I think the floodwaters got her," the woman said, waving around a picture of her sister. "I've lost my best friend."

"You're safe," Roberts said. "You're going to be OK."

On another rescue mission, Roberts helped a woman into the boat as the evacuee said, "Please don't let them leave my boy!"

"Where is your son?" Roberts asked.

"He died in the attic. He was sick, and it was so, so hot. He couldn't breathe."

Roberts comforted the woman as she explained that they couldn't go into the house and try to get her son's body.

Later that day, Roberts was amazed to find the lost sister of the woman she had helped in the day's first mission. She was able to reunite the two women, each of whom had thought the other had died. In a day filled with pain and suffering, Roberts was grateful for a happy moment.

Roberts, Lovett, and the Cajun Navy continued their rescue missions throughout the day. That night, they put the boats back on trailers and slept in their trucks. The next day would probably bring more heartache and joy.

Vien The Nguyen
August 31, Mary Queen of Vietnam Church, New Orleans

People kept coming to the church seeking shelter. Father Nguyen figured about 200 people must be there by now. Food was running low, but someone had used a boat to bring a drowned deer to the church. Nguyen and some others prepared it for a barbecue. Some evacuees had brought food from home, so they grilled that too.

In the afternoon, Nguyen was trying to nap when he heard a knock.

"Someone is here to see you, Father," a voice said. Nguyen went to the door and saw an unfamiliar man.

"Can I help you?" Nguyen asked.

"I'm here to help you," the man said. "We have boats—big boats from the Wildlife and Fishery Department. We're here to rescue you."

Nguyen's initial joy faded a bit when he remembered the sick, elderly parishioner upstairs. He explained the situation to the man and they agreed that only a medical helicopter could get her out. In addition, the woman had a daughter in a wheelchair.

"Take everyone else you can," Nguyen said. "I'll stay here with the family."

Soon everyone was gone except Nguyen and the family of the sick woman. He made calls to people he knew in government, to see if they could arrange for a helicopter. But by the end of the day, none had arrived.

Throughout the day, boats came to the hospital and took away more patients. Some were airboats, with giant fans that pushed them across the water. They could only carry a few people at a time. Karen Wynn helped decide who would go first. Then she and other nurses tried to help the people left behind. They sat in wheelchairs and waited for their turn.

A man she didn't recognize as a patient came to the ramp where people were waiting. A long tube trailed from his body.

"I have liver disease, I need treatment," the man said.

"Where did you come from?" Wynn asked, seeing his soaked pants.

"I walked from my house," he said.

Wynn shook her head. She knew he had waded through water that was dirty and filled with bacteria. He could get a serious infection on top of his liver disease. She called out to a doctor, "He's gotta go. He's gotta go on the next boat."

As darkness fell and the last boat pulled away, Wynn helped wheel patients who hadn't been rescued back into the dark, hot hospital. Inside they were greeted by the stink of toilets that had backed up. The hospital staff also worried about looters, and an official passed out guns some employees had brought from home.

Wynn gathered together her nurses and explained that about 115 patients were still in the hospital.

"We need volunteers to take care of them through the night," she said.

In response, most of her staff said they had already realized that and were ready to stay.

"I just want to say how proud I am of all of you," Wynn said, struggling to hold back tears. "I know how difficult this is and how hard you've worked."

ON THE BUS AND IN THE CITY

5

Hurricane Katrina survivors at the Astrodome in
Houston, Texas, after being evacuated from New Orleans

Jabbar had gotten behind the wheel of another bus with gas, and now he and Courtney Miles drove the buses back to their neighborhood. Nas rode with Miles.

"Nas," Miles said, "I don't believe we really got these buses."

"I just hope we don't get arrested," Nas said. "We're taking a bus."

"This is an emergency," Miles said. "We're going to rescue people!"

Miles tried to be confident, but he worried about staying safe on the road. The streets were flooded, and he hoped he wouldn't hit something and get a flat tire. But both buses made it, and the people of the neighborhood cheered when they saw Miles and Jabbar pull up. The neighbors realized they were going to be able to leave.

Soon several hundred people jammed into the buses, carrying their belongings in plastic bags and pillowcases. Miles pulled out and headed for the highway. He said a prayer to himself, thanking God for helping them find the buses and keys. And he prayed for a safe journey out of New Orleans.

The buses continued until they reached the highway ramp. Two police cars blocked the way and one officer motioned for them to stop. Without a license, Miles knew they would never let him keep going. But he was determined to get his passengers to safety. He jerked the wheel to the right, taking the bus down a street that ran along the highway.

"I think you should stop," one woman said.

But other passengers began to chant, "Go, go, go!"

Miles kept going—and he was relieved when he realized that neither of the police cars was coming after him. He found another way onto the highway and someone asked, "Just where are we going, anyway?"

Miles hadn't thought of that. But the word "Lafayette" popped into his head, so that's where he said they were heading—the city of Lafayette, about 130 miles away.

As he drove, Miles realized the second bus was no longer following him. He hoped Jabbar made it out of the city all right. Miles stopped several times along the way to pick up more people. The passengers groaned—they were already packed in tight. Soon Miles realized he couldn't pick up any more passengers, though he kept seeing people in need of help. He promised himself he would come back for them, somehow.

Miles didn't see any other cars for a long time—until someone pointed out one ahead. "It's a sheriff's car!" someone said. Miles just kept driving, eventually passing the slower car. Miles saw the sheriff look surprised, but then the man just smiled and nodded. Miles smiled back and kept driving.

After several hours, he pulled his bus in front of an arena called the Cajundome. He didn't know for sure, but Miles had hoped the arena was being used as a shelter for evacuees. And he was right. Soon his almost 200 passengers filed off the bus and headed for food and showers. When he got off the bus, Miles was surprised to see that Troy Moody, a friend from New Orleans, was already there.

"Good to see you, Courtney," Moody said. "Your grandmother was asking today if I might know—"

"My grandmother?" Miles asked in disbelief. "She's here? She's OK?"

"Yeah, she's here. And she's fine."

Miles tried to run into the building, but a guard stopped him and told him to wait in line with the others. Miles tried to argue his way past, but the guard was firm. Finally, Miles got in line. But he knew that soon he would see his grandmother. She spied him as he stood in line and came over to give him a hug.

"How'd you get here?" he asked her.

"Your uncle took me," his grandmother said. "How did you get here?"

Miles hesitated. "Well, I, ah, came with some of my friends."

"You're shaking," his grandmother said. "Did you do something you shouldn't do?"

"No, grandma." He said, not wanting to tell her about the buses.

"I don't believe you," she said. "But come on. Let me get you some food."

After eating some pizza, Miles slipped away from his grandmother and climbed back into the bus. He had promised himself that he would help the people he left behind on the road, and he headed back toward New Orleans to find them. He reached New Orleans and found the people he was looking for. Before long he found a second group looking to leave the city. Miles felt like an old hand now as a bus driver. A little after midnight, he returned to the Cajundome with another 100 or so people who were happy to be out of their flooded hometown.

Residents wait for help outside the convention center in downtown New Orleans.

Ivory Clark

Early on Thursday, Ivory Clark had found a safer spot for his family in a parking lot near the convention center. In the morning, he knew he once again had to find food for his family. He sometimes cooked for a wealthy white family that lived nearby. Clark took his son, Gerald, with him and set off for their building.

Outside the building, a police officer stood guard. He pointed a rifle at the father and son.

"Where are you going?" the officer asked.

"Look, I live here," Clark said, hoping to get inside any way he could.

Just then, two security guards who worked at the building spotted Clark. They recognized him and told the officer it was OK for Clark and Gerald to enter.

Clark had a key to the condo of the family he worked for. It seemed that they had fled the city, but he was relieved to find that a generator had kept their refrigerator running. Clark was soon cooking up all the food he could find. When it was ready, he and Gerald brought the food back to the rest of the family and others near them in the parking lot.

But Clark's work wasn't done. He still needed a generator for his aunt's breathing machine. He went into the convention center, approached a National Guard member, and explained the situation.

"Yeah, we have generators," the soldier said. "But they're for official use only. Sorry."

Clark left the center, and his family prepared to spend another night sleeping in the parking lot. Pieces of cardboard provided their only comfort against the hard pavement.

Peter Ward

Peter Ward continued his almost nonstop rescue work. Now traveling with firefighters, he went to the parts of the city that had experienced the most flooding. Some people were in the flooded streets, while others sat on their roofs. Perhaps remembering the flooding from Hurricane Betsy, some had brought axes with them to chop through the wood and shingles.

On one rescue, a large woman jumped from a roof into the boat. Her weight made the boat push away from the house. A man still on the roof began to panic. "Don't go without me!" he cried. He tried to leap into the boat but missed. Ward saw the ring of water that formed where he went in. With a long pole, Ward prodded the water, offering something the man could hold onto. When he couldn't find the man, Ward dropped the pole and reached over the boat to search with his hand. As he leaned over, Ward almost went into the water himself. Stretching as far as he could, Ward finally found the man's shoulder.

"Help me!" he called.

Someone else in the boat helped Ward pull up the man. At first he didn't seem to be breathing, but as the man hit against the side of the boat a fountain of water flew out of his mouth. After that he began breathing again. They left the man and the others on high ground and then went back for another rescue mission.

In the days after Katrina, hundreds of volunteers joined the effort to rescue people who had been stranded by floodwaters.

Karen Wynn

September 1, Memorial Medical Center, New Orleans

On Thursday morning, Karen Wynn helped more patients get onto the boats. Some were also being evacuated by helicopter. But everyone had to be out that day. The police officers guarding the hospital said the area was becoming too dangerous. They said looters were still out all over the city, and some carried guns.

As someone who worked in intensive care, Wynn knew doctors and nurses could not save everyone. Sometimes people died despite receiving the best medical care. Now she took inventory of the sickest patients still in the hospital. Some were struggling to breathe. Without life support machines and with such bad conditions in the hospital, some of these people were close to death. Other patients were at a point where there was no way Wynn or the doctors could save them.

Wynn knew what was important now was for the staff to do what they could to keep these patients from suffering. She and other nurses passed out drugs to try to make the sickest patients as comfortable as possible.

Courtney Miles
September 1, Lafayette, Louisiana

A huge TV constantly played the news inside the Cajundome. Late the night before, someone shouted that Courtney Miles's friend Jabbar was on CNN. He had taken his bus all the way to Houston, Texas. Miles was glad to hear he had made it out of New Orleans. But today another news report worried him. President George W. Bush was speaking about the situation. Bush said, "I think there ought to be zero tolerance of people breaking the law during an emergency such as this."

Miles was scared. Did that mean he would be arrested for taking the bus? He imagined himself being led away in handcuffs. Every time he saw a police officer or National Guard member, he panicked. But he had nowhere to go. He just waited and hoped nothing would happen to him.

Vien The Nguyen
September 1, Mary Queen of Vietnam Church, New Orleans

Father Nguyen looked out and saw some of the parishioners who had left the day before coming back to the church. They told him that the rescuers had taken them to high ground near a highway and told them to wait for someone to take them to the Superdome or the convention center. The rescuers had said that the Red Cross would provide food. But none of that happened. Nguyen's people had waited out there all night.

Someone with a boat was able to take Nguyen to the scene. He was relieved to see that military trucks were taking the people off the high ground. But back at the church, there was still no sign of a medevac helicopter to rescue his sick parishioner.

Nguyen made more calls. "The gas for the generator is really low," he said. "We only have one more day."

Warren Riley
September 2, New Orleans

A little after midnight on Friday, Warren Riley drove up to a highway that cut through New Orleans. It was on high ground, and people rescued from their homes gathered there to wait for rides to the convention center or Superdome. Riley figured there had to be 600 people there.

When he heard that dozens of National Guard trucks had reached the convention center, Riley drove over to ask for help. He said to one of the Guard members, "We've got all these people stranded on the interstate; they've had no water all day. We need 10 to 12 of your trucks."

The soldier said he had to ask his general. When he returned, he told Riley that his general wouldn't grant the request. Riley couldn't believe it and asked to talk to the general himself. The soldier said, "The general has already spoken."

Angry and frustrated, Riley scanned the street and saw a man driving by in a big truck. He motioned for the driver to stop, and he did. Riley told the driver he needed his truck and was going to take it from him. When Riley explained the situation, the driver said he would volunteer to help. All morning, Riley watched the man go back and forth between the highway and the convention center, carrying hundreds of wet and thirsty evacuees. To Riley, the man was a hero.

Some residents took shelter on bridges and overpasses to escape the floodwaters.

Karen Wynn

Karen Wynn and about 50 other people had spent the night around the helipad on top of Memorial Medical Center. Afraid of looters, they decided they were safer outside. A few staff members with guns guarded the entrance to the outside area.

When Friday morning came, the rescue helicopters returned. Wynn got on one, which took her to the city airport. It seemed that, for her, the worst of Katrina was finally over. She thought she and her nurses had done the best they could under almost impossible conditions.

Renee Martin

September 2, Superdome,
New Orleans

In the morning Renee Martin saw soldiers entering the Superdome. She saw that they were carrying guns and fear flashed through her. She wondered if they were going to kill everyone there.

"Please put the guns down," she told several soldiers nearby. "All we want to do is get out of here."

"Ma'am," one soldier replied, "We're here to rescue y'all."

The soldiers took her and some others outside. Above them, large helicopters lowered down baskets.

"Get in, ma'am," a soldier said.

"I'm scared!" Martin cried.

"You'll be fine."

Soon Martin was on the high ground along the highway, along with many others.

The Red Cross was there offering real food, not the military MREs that had been served in the Superdome. But Martin was too nervous to eat, so she had an energy drink instead.

Later in the day, Martin could see school buses driving toward her and the others.

"They're for us," someone cried. "They're going to take us to Baton Rouge." That city, the capital of Louisiana, had missed most of Katrina's deadly punch. The people around Martin rushed toward a bus with its door open. But a sheriff stepped forward.

"You have to go in order," he said. "There are people ahead of you who have been waiting longer. There will be more buses."

The crowd stepped back and waited, but no more buses came that day. Martin prepared to spend the night outside, with all the others still waiting to be rescued.

Vien The Nguyen

By 11:00 a.m., Father Nguyen still had
no sign that anyone was coming to rescue the
sick woman. Sadness filled her husband, who
said, "Father, I don't think anyone is coming
to rescue us."

"Don't lose hope yet," Nguyen said. "Let
me make another call."

As Nguyen prepared to make more calls,
he heard the sound of motors outside. A boat
with several men on board pulled up. The
boat was big enough to carry the woman, her
family, and the priest. The men took them
to trucks on dry land nearby. They carefully
placed the woman on one of the trucks so
they could go look for an ambulance. The
woman's son went with her. Meanwhile,
another of the men agreed to take Nguyen
and the others to Lafayette.

Driving through New Orleans to the highway, Nguyen saw buildings that had been destroyed. One house was on fire after a gas pipeline exploded near it. And people gathered on high ground, dazed from all the suffering they had experienced.

Nguyen stayed with another priest in Lafayette. Late that night, he took his first shower in five days. Afterward, he joked to the other priest, "I almost drowned in there. It's been so long, I didn't know how to do it."

Vien The Nguyen with his congregation in the storm-damaged church

GOOD NEWS, BAD NEWS

6

New Orleans was flooded for weeks after Hurricane Katrina hit the city.

Warren Riley

Warren Riley had continued to get reports about officers stuck in their homes, along with other residents of New Orleans. He also heard reports of shootings. Early on Saturday morning, he was in the Emergency Center at City Hall when a call came in about a possible shooting at the convention center. Riley entered a room where cots had been set up so that officers could rest or take naps. Sitting on one of the cots was Officer Paul Accardo.

"It never stops," Riley said.

"Yeah, Chief, it never stops," Accardo replied.

To Riley, the officer seemed down. Like many others, Accardo had lost his house. He had also spent long days trying to rescue people, and even animals. Riley left him to head to the convention center. He knew he would have to find a way to stay focused. New Orleans was still struggling.

Renee Martin

Still waiting along the highway, Renee Martin woke up on Saturday to see a new line of buses. They were waiting to evacuate people. A man came over to her and said, "You're on bus 6, and it's going to Texas."

When it was time to board, people began to push and shove, but Martin held her ground. She was determined to get on that bus. When she did, she took a seat behind the driver.

As the bus pulled away, Martin waved to TV cameras outside. With each mile that passed, she felt a little more relaxed, especially when she saw the sign welcoming her to Texas. When they reached the Houston Astrodome, the victims of Katrina found food, clothing, showers—even toys for the children. Martin thought she might stay in Houston and start a new life.

Peter Ward

By Saturday, the water was starting to recede in some parts of New Orleans. Peter Ward had continued rescuing people throughout Friday, but now he thought he should check on how well his house had survived Katrina. On the way, he picked up about 130 people who wanted to go to Jefferson Parish, where he lived. It was his last rescue mission.

At home, Ward found that some water had gotten into the house, but it had dried. None of the water had affected the things he needed for his business, so he was glad of that. Ward thought about all he had experienced. He felt a bond with the police and firefighters he had worked with, trying to help others. He knew he would never experience anything like it again.

Sara Roberts

Sara Roberts waited for word from her husband. The Cajun Navy had returned to Lake Charles on Thursday, after spending the night not far from the convention center. When Ronny Lovett heard reports of violence in the area, he thought the volunteers should return home. But now, on Saturday, they had ventured into New Orleans again. Roberts, though, had gotten sick after the first rescue mission, so she missed this second day. But she knew the Cajun Navy was once again helping people in need.

Ivory Clark

On Saturday morning, Ivory Clark and his family stood outside the convention center, waiting for food and water. Clark was glad his 91-year-old mother-in-law was still doing pretty well, but his aunt was suffering from her asthma. Later in the morning, people lined up for buses that would take them out of the city. Clark wanted to be sure his family got out as soon as possible.

When buses started pulling up to the building, Clark headed to the last ones, not the first. He knew everyone would try to scramble to be first in line. He approached a member of the National Guard and explained the situation with his sick aunt and elderly mother-in-law. "Can't we get on one of these buses?" Clark pleaded. "We've got to stay together as a family."

To Clark's delight the Guard member told Clark to get everyone together. "Come on," the soldier said. "You're going in the sky."

Soon Clark found out that helicopters were coming to evacuate sick people. Now his family moved into the line for people waiting to fly out. When the word came, they bent down under the whirring blades and got ready for their first helicopter ride.

Up in the air, Clark looked down over the flooded city. He looked for his neighborhood and realized the streets there had water about 8 feet deep. Clark began to cry. But he knew now that the family he had worked so hard to protect was going to be all right. The helicopter was taking them to an airport, where doctors would take care of his aunt. Then, they would head to a shelter in Baton Rouge.

The thought went through his mind again. *We're going to be all right.*

Thousands of people waited outside of the Superdome,
hoping to be evacuated from the city.

Courtney Miles

Courtney Miles continued to sweat whenever he saw anyone in a uniform. Someone had moved the bus from the arena, but officials could still be looking for whoever took it from New Orleans to Lafayette. But several days had passed and no one had asked him any questions. Maybe he would be all right.

Living for days in the Cajundome had not been easy. About 1,000 people slept together in an open space, and Miles struggled to sleep as babies cried and adults snored or talked to the people around them. But he would be leaving soon. His grandmother had signed up for one of the trailers that FEMA was providing to some people who had evacuated New Orleans. Miles thought about going back to New Orleans and finishing high school. He wondered what life would be like after Katrina.

EPILOGUE

A week after Katrina hit New Orleans, Warren Riley stood in front of reporters and said, "We advise people that this city has been destroyed." Almost all the people who had stayed in New Orleans during the storm had now left the flooded city. Riley encouraged the few thousand who remained to seek dry land. He said that citizens with boats who wanted to help with rescue efforts were welcome, but asked that they work with the city rather than on their own.

Riley also addressed the question of why more police hadn't been available to help in the days after Katrina. He explained that 400 to 500 officers were not accounted for. Some left for various reasons. "Some of those officers," Riley said, "lost their homes; they don't know where their families are; where their spouses are, and they're out looking for them; some left because they simply could not deal with this catastrophe." Riley added, "This was probably the greatest catastrophe in an American city."

The final numbers on Katrina highlight the size of that catastrophe. In all, more than 1,800 people died because of the storm, and it caused more than $135 billion in damages. Some of the dead were never identified and family members never claimed their bodies. The year after the storm, the population of New Orleans and the surrounding area had fallen by more than 200,000. Many people who had fled Katrina never returned. By 2014, though, the area's population had risen, though it still did not reach the number who lived there before Katrina.

In Washington, D.C., lawmakers in Congress wanted to know what the National Hurricane Center had done in the days before Katrina. They wanted to know what meteorologists could do in the future to provide better forecasts. Max Mayfield did not speak directly to Congress, but he sent a written statement that was dated September 20, 2005.

In his statement, Mayfield described how accurately he and his staff predicted Katrina's path in the Gulf of Mexico. He outlined the warnings the center gave. He also discussed the possibility of other deadly storms. He wrote, "Katrina will not be the last major hurricane to hit a vulnerable area, and New Orleans is not the only location vulnerable to a large disaster from a land-falling hurricane. Houston/Galveston, Tampa Bay, southwest Florida, Florida Keys, southeast Florida, New York City/Long Island, and believe it or not, New England, are all especially vulnerable. And New Orleans remains vulnerable to future hurricanes."

A month later, Marty Bahamonde spoke to members of the U.S. Senate. They wanted to know what FEMA had done before and during Katrina. Bahamonde described his actions from when he arrived in New Orleans until he left. He said, "From this [hearing] I hope that we are able to effect change so that no other child, no other senior citizen, no other special needs patient, no other parent, and no other community in this country will ever have to experience the horrors and tragedy that happened in New Orleans and the entire Gulf Coast that week."

In 2015, the people of New Orleans marked the tenth anniversary of Katrina in different ways. Some went to memorial services to honor the dead. Others took part in volunteer activities across the city. A parade went through one part of the city that had been badly damaged, to show the recovery efforts still going on. The U.S. government had helped the city's recovery by spending billions of dollars to build new floodgates and pumps in New Orleans. Other projects continue to build new flood control systems and fortifications to protect southern Louisiana from future hurricanes.

Just before the tenth anniversary, President Barack Obama visited New Orleans. On August 29, he tweeted this message from the city's Tremé neighborhood: "In Tremé, I was inspired by the progress & people 10 years after Katrina. It gives us hope, but our work isn't done."

TIMELINE

August 23, 2005: The National Hurricane Center issues its first advisory about the tropical weather system that will become Hurricane Katrina.

August 24: The weather system strengthens and is named tropical storm Katrina.

August 25: Katrina continues to strengthen and is upgraded to a Category 1 hurricane.

August 26: Hurricane Katrina enters the Gulf of Mexico and gains strength as it heads toward New Orleans; states of emergency are declared in Louisiana and Mississippi.

August 27: Louisiana governor Kathleen Blanco tells residents in low-lying areas near the Gulf Coast to evacuate, but the order is not mandatory.

August 28: Max Mayfield of the National Hurricane Center informs the Federal Emergency Management Agency that Katrina is now a Category 5 storm and is on track to hit New Orleans; the city's mayor, Ray Nagin, orders a mandatory evacuation but many residents remain in New Orleans; the Superdome opens for people who want to leave their homes but can't leave the city.

August 29: Katrina makes landfall around 6:00 a.m., with winds reaching 145 miles per hour; later in the morning, the first of several levees breaches, filling parts of New Orleans with water; residents continue to flock to the Superdome, which lost power during the storm, while others now go to the Morial Convention Center; looters begin to rob whatever they can take from closed stores.

August 30: Some hospitals begin evacuating patients as floodwater continues to rise in parts of the city; people with boats try to rescue people trapped in their homes.

August 31: For the first time, the media reports on the horrible conditions at the convention center; volunteers from outside New Orleans come to rescue stranded people.

September 1: The first buses arrive to take people out of the Superdome; President George W. Bush condemns the crime that has occurred in New Orleans.

September 2: National Guard soldiers begin passing out food and water to people at the Superdome and convention center; President Bush signs a bill approving $10.5 billion in aid for Hurricane Katrina rescue and relief.

September 3: Buses and helicopters arrive to take people from the convention center; some evacuees go to other parts of Louisiana, while others go to Texas.

September 5: Most people who remained in New Orleans through Katrina have now left, because of the flooding and lack of public services, such as water and electricity; an estimated 134,000 housing units in New Orleans were damaged, and tens of thousands of people who left the city never returned.

GLOSSARY

breach (BREECH)—an opening or a gap in a structure

Cajun (KAY-juhn)—a descendant of the French Acadians of eastern Canada

commission (kuh-MI-shun)—group of people who plan or run some kind of government operation

dike (DYK)—a strong wall built to keep water from flooding the land

evacuate (i-VA-kyuh-wayt)—to leave an area during a time of danger

Gulf Coast (GUHLF KOHST)—the part of the United States that borders the Gulf of Mexico

levee (LEV-ee)—embankment built to prevent a body of water from overflowing

loot (LOOT)—to steal from stores or houses during wartime or after a disaster

mandatory (MAN-duh-tor-ee)—required by someone in authority or a government

meteorologist (mee-tee-ur-AWL-uh-jist)—a person who studies and predicts the weather

parish (PA-rish)—word used in Louisiana to describe sections of land that would be called counties in other states; also an area or group of people that has its own church minister or priest

parishioners (pa-RISH-uhn-uhrs)—the people who attend a particular church

storm surge (STORM SURJ)—a sudden, strong rush of water that happens as a hurricane moves onto land

ultrasound (UHL-truh-sound)—a medical device that takes images inside the body

videographer (VID-ee-ah-gra-fuhr)—a person who records images with a video camera

vulnerable (VUHL-nur-uh-buhl)—in a weak position and likely to be hurt or damaged in some way

CRITICAL THINKING USING THE COMMON CORE

1. What factors about Katrina worried Max Mayfield as he tracked the storm? (Key Ideas and Details)

2. Why did the New Orleans police force have several hundred officers not available to help when the storm hit? (Key Ideas and Details)

3. Some people in New Orleans broke the law to help themselves and their families survive. Find an example of this and explain why it was or was not justified for the person to do what they did. (Integration of Knowledge and Ideas)

INTERNET SITES

FactHound offers a safe, fun way to find Internet sites related to this book. All of the sites on FactHound have been researched by our staff.

Here's all you do:
Visit *www.facthound.com*
Type in this code: 9781491484524

FactHound will fetch the best sites for you!

FURTHER READING

Bjorklund, Ruth, and Andy Steinitz. *Louisiana*. New York: Cavendish Square, 2015.

Hoena, Blake. *Hurricane Katrina: An Interactive Modern History Adventure*. North Mankato, Minn.: Capstone Press, 2014.

Koontz, Robin. *What Was Hurricane Katrina?* New York: Grosset & Dunlap, An Imprint of Penguin Random House, 2015.

Langley, Andrew. *Hurricane: Perspectives on Storm Disasters*. Chicago: Raintree, 2015.

Reina, Mary. *The Science of a Hurricane*. Ann Arbor, Mich.: Cherry Lake Publishing, 2015.

Tuchman, Gail. *Hurricane Katrina*. New York: Scholastic, Inc., 2015.

SELECTED BIBLIOGRAPHY

Antoine, Rebeca, ed. *Voices Rising: Stories from the Katrina Narrative Project*. New Orleans: UNO Press, 2008.

Brinkley, Douglas. *The Great Deluge: Hurricane Katrina, New Orleans, and the Mississippi Gulf Coast*. New York: Morrow, 2006.

Fink, Sheri. *Five Days at Memorial: Life and Death in a Storm-Ravaged Hospital*. New York: Crown Publishers, 2013.

McDowell, Beck. *Last Bus Out: The True Story of Courtney Miles' Rescue of Over 300 People in Hurricane Katrina's Aftermath*. Kindle version. N.p.: Kirkland & Fort, 2010.

Vollen, Lola, and Chris Ying, eds. *Voices from the Storm: The People of New Orleans on Hurricane Katrina and Its Aftermath*. San Francisco: McSweeney's Books, 2006.

INDEX

ABOUT THE AUTHOR

Michael Burgan is a freelance writer who specializes in books for children and young adults, both fiction and nonfiction. A graduate of the University of Connecticut with a degree in history, Burgan is also a produced playwright and the editor of *The Biographer's Craft*, the newsletter for Biographers International Organization. He lives in Santa Fe, New Mexico.